King Arthur
and the Legend of Excalibur

*The Tale of the Sword of Camelot and
the Knights of the Round Table*

I0408298

an Adult Coloring Book by Tes Scholtz

Artwork Anywhere ™
Classics

Medieval Stories to color: Volume 1

King Arthur
and the Legend of Excalibur

The Tale of the Sword of Camelot and the Knights of the Round Table

an Adult Coloring Book by Tes Scholtz

King Arthur and the Legend of Excalibur adult coloring book features 25 hand drawn illustrations that tell the tale of the sword of Camelot and the knights of the round table.

King Uther, Guinevere, Lancelot, the Lady of the Lake, and the great Merlin all make appearances.

Artwork Anywhere Classics is a series of classic stories and folklore retold with new illustrations for you to color. Written and illustrated by Tes Scholtz.

Use colored pencils, crayons, inks, gel pens, markers, whatever you want, or mix it up and use them all! There are no rules. There are suggestions, though: Some markers and paints may bleed through the pages. To avoid damaging other pages, use a barrier sheet between pages, or remove the page from the book before coloring.

All of my coloring books are printed single-sided, so you don't have to worry about colors showing through the back side, or smudging against each other face-to-face. Plus, no more deciding which side you like better if you want to remove it from the book.

Artwork Anywhere™
Classics
Medieval Stories to color: Volume 1

ArtworkAnywhere.com

ArtworkAnywhere.com

Arthur is the firstborn son to King Uther Pendragon.
He was born in secret, into troubled times in the kingdom.

The great sorcerer Merlin was worried for the baby's well-being, and brought the child to be secretly raised by Sir Ector.

Arthur grows up with Ector's son, Kay. They are raised as brothers.

Upon King Uther's death, there is great debate over who should rule the kingdom.

ArtworkAnywhere.com

Merlin sets a magical sword into a great stone, declaring that he who can pull the sword from the stone shall be king. The sword is called Excalibur.

ArtworkAnywhere.com

Over the years, many attempt to pull the sword from the stone, but they all fail.

One day, Kay and Arthur attend a jousting tournament together. Kay's sword goes missing.

ArtworkAnywhere.com

They are passing near the sword in the stone, unaware of the story behind it. Arthur sees the sword and thinks to replace Kay's sword with it.

ArtworkAnywhere.com

Arthur easily pulls the sword from the stone, to the astonishment of the nearby jousters.

ArtworkAnywhere.com

Merlin arrives to announce Arthur's true identity, and his right to be king. Arthur is not sure what to think of this.

Having been declared King, Arthur must learn to master his magical new sword.

Merlin is wise and knows much about the kingdom and its people. He stays with Arthur, to train, advise, and mentor him.

Arthur gathers together the best knights to protect the kingdom, and battle the Saxons.

They had many great battles and emerged victorious, defeating the Saxons at Mount Badon.

ArtworkAnywhere.com

Arthur encounters the undefeated knight Lancelot, who demands combat with Arthur, to prove the king's worthiness.

Arthur summons Excalibur's magic to prove his superiority. He defeats Lancelot, but in doing so, he breaks the sword Excalibur.

ArtworkAnywhere.com

Ashamed at his own actions, Arthur admits his wrongdoing while casting the pieces of Excalibur into the lake.

The Lady of the Lake restores the sword, and offers it back to Arthur.

Arthur humbly accepts the sword,
and Lancelot is revived.

With his mighty weapon restored, Arthur learns to respect his own powers, and the strength of his sword. He realizes all that he must do as King.

ArtworkAnywhere.com

Arthur built a great castle at Camelot and chose the beautiful Guinevere to become his Queen.

He met with his
Knights at the legendary Round Table.

ArtworkAnywhere.com

The King and his Knights were chivalrous, rescuing damsels in distress, and treating all the people of Camelot fairly, and with kindness.

They battled strange and fantastic
beasts throughout the lands, and
vanquished many foes.

ArtworkAnywhere.com

What wondrous adventures lie ahead for King Arthur and his kingdom?